# MIGUEL CABRERA
## MVP AND TRIPLE CROWN WINNER

BY BRENDAN FLYNN

Published by The Child's World®
1980 Lookout Drive • Mankato, MN 56003-1705
800-599-READ • www.childsworld.com

ACKNOWLEDGMENTS
The Child's World®: Mary Berendes, Publishing Director
Red Line Editorial: Editorial direction
The Design Lab: Design
Amnet: Production
Design Elements: Open Clip Art Library
Photographs ©: Andrew Woolley/AP Images, cover; Photo
Works/Shutterstock Images, 5; Alejandro Cegarra/AP Images,
7; Tony Gutierrez/AP Images, 9; Four Seam Images/AP Images,
11; Vick McKenzie/Corbis Images, 13; Alan Diaz/AP Images,
15; Paul Sancya/AP Images, 17; Scott W. Grau/Icon SMI, 19;
Kydpl Kyodo/AP Images, 21

ISBN 9781631437366
LCCN 2014945305

Printed in the United States of America
Mankato, MN
November, 2014
PA02239

## ABOUT THE AUTHOR

Brendan Flynn is a San Francisco resident and author of numerous children's books. In addition to writing about sports, Flynn also enjoys competing in triathlons, Scrabble tournaments, and chili cook-offs.

# TABLE OF CONTENTS

# CHAPTER 1

# POWERHOUSE AT THE PLATE

It is the bottom of the ninth inning. The Detroit Tigers need a big hit. They are losing by a run. But there are two runners on base. Then Miguel Cabrera steps up to the plate. The situation is made for a clutch hitter like Cabrera. The pitcher fires his best fastball. The bat cracks, and the ball sails into the seats in left field. It's a home run, and the Tigers win. Cabrera has done it again.

Through 2013 Cabrera had hit six "walk-off" home runs. That means he hit a home run to end a game.

*Cabrera steps up to bat against the Los Angeles Dodgers on June 20, 2011.*

# CHAPTER 2

# EARLY YEARS

On April 18, 1983, Jose Miguel Torres Cabrera was born in Maracay, Venezuela. His father was a star **amateur** player. His mother was the shortstop for the Venezuelan national softball team. Miguel grew up around the ballpark.

Many great baseball players have come from Venezuela. Miguel's hero growing up was Dave Concepcion. Concepcion was the longtime shortstop for the Cincinnati Reds.

Miguel's uncle, David, played minor-league baseball in the United States. Miguel wanted to be like his uncle. David helped Miguel develop his talent. Their hard work paid off. Miguel became a powerful hitter. As he grew, his skills drew the attention of major-league scouts.

Another of Cabrera's uncles, Jose Torres, runs a baseball academy on the field where Cabrera learned to play in Maracay, Venezuela.

# CHAPTER 3

# BIDDING WAR

**M**iguel did not live in the United States. That meant he was not eligible for the Major League Baseball (MLB) Draft. Teams send scouts to countries where baseball is popular. Scouts look for talented players. Once a foreign player turns 16, he can sign a **contract** with an MLB team.

Miguel was almost 17 when he went to his first training camp. He was already 6'2" and 185 pounds!

Many teams wanted to sign Miguel. But his favorite team was the Florida Marlins. The Marlins offered Miguel $1.8 million to sign with them. Other teams offered as much as $2 million. But Miguel wanted to play for the Marlins. He signed a contract with Florida. His baseball dreams were close to coming true.

*Miguel was 16 years old on August 4, 1999, when it was announced that the Florida Marlins had signed him.*

# CHAPTER 4

# CLIMBING THE LADDER

Cabrera started in the minor leagues to improve his skills. He showed that he could hit for a high **batting average**. He could also drive the ball deep to all parts of the ballpark. That is a rare skill for a player as young as Cabrera.

Cabrera twice represented the Marlins at the MLB Futures Game. The game features the top minor-league **prospects** in all of baseball.

Cabrera was rated the twelfth-best prospect in the minor leagues by *Baseball America* magazine after the 2002 season.

*Cabrera stands ready at shortstop for the minor league Utica Blue Sox on July 31, 2000.*

# CHAPTER 5

# CHANGING POSITIONS

Cabrera was always a great hitter. His defense was another story. He started his career as a shortstop. But he was too big and bulky to play the position well.

Third base proved to be a better fit for Cabrera. He could relax and focus on his hitting.

Cabrera began the 2003 season with the Double-A Carolina Mudcats. Double-A baseball is just two steps below the majors. Cabrera was 20 years old. But he knew he was ready to hit major-league pitching. Then he got the call that changed his life forever.

Cabrera hit .402 for the Mudcats that April. By June he was hitting .365 with 10 home runs.

*Cabrera got four hits as a Marlin against the San Francisco Giants on October 4, 2003.*

# CHAPTER 6

# SURPRISE CALL-UP

The 2003 Marlins had plenty of talented players. But they started out slow. By mid-June the Marlins decided they needed something new. They called up Cabrera. He was their top prospect in the minors. Cabrera impressed the Marlins in his very first game. He hit a walk-off home run to beat the Tampa Bay Devil Rays.

The hits kept coming. In 87 games that year, Cabrera hit .268 with 12 home runs. His first year in the major leagues ended with a World Series championship for the Marlins. And their 20-year-old **rookie** was a big part of the victory.

Cabrera was the sixth-youngest player to hit a home run in his first MLB game.

*Cabrera runs the bases after his game-winning home run in his debut with the Marlins on June 20, 2003.*

# CHAPTER 7

# MOVING TO DETROIT

Cabrera spent five seasons with the Marlins. He was a National League **All-Star** four times. He won two Silver Slugger awards as the best hitter at his position. But the Marlins were not winning. Most of the veterans from the World Series team had retired or moved on to other teams. The Marlins decided to rebuild with young players. They traded Cabrera and pitcher Dontrelle Willis to Detroit for six minor-league prospects.

In 2005 Cabrera became the youngest player to hit 30 home runs in two straight seasons.

On March 31, 2008, Cabrera played his first game for the Detroit Tigers. He hit a home run in his third at-bat as a Tiger. Cabrera led the American League (AL) with 37 home runs that year.

*Cabrera throws to first during his first game as a Tiger on March 31, 2008.*

# CHAPTER 8

# TRIPLE CROWN WINNER

**T**he Tigers missed the playoffs in Cabrera's first three seasons in Detroit. In 2011 they made the AL Championship Series but lost to the Texas Rangers. In 2012 Cabrera led the AL with 44 home runs, 139 runs batted in (RBIs), and a .330 batting average. He had led the league in each of those categories before. But never in the same season.

Leading the league in those three categories is called the Triple Crown. Cabrera was named the AL Most Valuable Player (MVP) after the 2012 season. He also helped the Tigers win the AL pennant. They lost to the San Francisco Giants in the World Series. But it was still an amazing season.

The last player to win a Triple Crown was Carl Yastrzemski of the Boston Red Sox in 1967.

*Cabrera throws to first after fielding a ground ball as third baseman for the Detroit Tigers on October 16, 2013, against the Boston Red Sox.*

# CHAPTER 9

# DOING IT AGAIN

Cabrera came back for more in the 2013 season. He won his second straight AL MVP Award. He did not win another Triple Crown, but his numbers were almost as good. He again hit 44 home runs and had 137 RBIs. His .348 batting average was the best of his career and gave him his third straight AL batting title. The Tigers won another AL Central division title, but they lost to the Boston Red Sox in the AL Championship Series.

Before the 2014 season, Cabrera signed a record-breaking contract with the Tigers. They agreed to pay him $292 million over the next 10 years. The Tigers know that as long as Cabrera is in their lineup, they have a good chance to win the World Series.

Cabrera and his wife, Rosangel, have three children. He started the Miguel Cabrera Foundation to help various charities and encourage kids to play baseball.

*Red Sox catcher David Ross tags out Cabrera during Game 5 of the AL Championship Series on October 17, 2013.*

# FUN FACTS

## MIGUEL CABRERA

**BORN:** April 18, 1983

**HOMETOWN:** Maracay, Venezuela

**TEAMS:** Florida Marlins (2003–07), Detroit Tigers (2007– )

**POSITIONS:** Third Baseman, First Baseman, Leftfielder

**HEIGHT:** 6′11″

**WEIGHT:** 240 pounds

**MAJOR LEAGUE DEBUT:** June 20, 2003

**ALL-STAR APPEARANCES:** 2004, 2005, 2006, 2007, 2010, 2011, 2012, 2013, 2014

**WORLD SERIES (WINS IN BOLD): 2003**, 2012

**AWARDS**

    **AL MVP:** 2012, 2013

    **AL BATTING TITLE:** 2011, 2012, 2013

    **AL HOME RUN TITLE:** 2008, 2012

    **AL RBI TITLE:** 2010, 2012

# GLOSSARY

**All-Star** (AWL stahr) A player who is named one of the best in the league is an All-Star. Cabrera was named an All-Star for the first time in 2004.

**amateur** (AM-uh-chur) An amateur is an athlete who is not paid to play a sport. Cabrera had a .348 batting average in the 2013 season.

**batting average** (BAT-ing AV-ur-ij) Batting average is a statistic that measures how often a player gets a base hit. A player with a batting average of .300 gets a hit three times in every 10 at-bats.

**contract** (KAHN-trakt) An agreement between a team and a player that determines years of service, salary, and other terms is a contract. Cabrera's contract with the Tigers is for $152.3 million over eight years.

**prospects** (PRAHS-pekts) Prospects are young players who have a good chance of becoming superstars. Cabrera was one of the top prospects in the minor leagues.

**rookie** (RUK-ee) A player in his or her first year in a new league is a rookie. Miguel Cabrera was a star rookie for the Marlins.

# TO LEARN MORE

## BOOKS

Detroit Free Press, The. *Days of Roar!: From Miguel Cabrera's Triple Crown to a Dynasty in the Making!* Chicago, IL: Triumph Books, 2013.

Green, David. *101 Reasons to Love the Tigers.* New York: Stewart, Tabori, and Chang, 2009.

LeBoutillier, Nate. *The Story of the Detroit Tigers.* Mankato, MN: Creative Paperbacks, 2012.

## WEB SITES

Visit our Web site for links about Miguel Cabrera:
### childsworld.com/links

*Note to Parents, Teachers, and Librarians: We routinely verify our Web links to make sure they are safe and active sites. So encourage your readers to check them out!*

# INDEX